# All in My Mind and No One Will Listen

Danny Cole

Copyright © 2000, 2012 Daniel Cole

All rights reserved. No part of this book may be used or reproduced by any means, graphic, electronic, or mechanical, including photocopying, recording, taping or by any information storage retrieval system without the written permission of the publisher except in the case of brief quotations embodied in critical articles and reviews.

Inspiring Voices books may be ordered through booksellers or by contacting:

Inspiring Voices
1663 Liberty Drive
Bloomington, IN 47403
www.inspiringvoices.com
1-(866) 697-5313

Because of the dynamic nature of the Internet, any web addresses or links contained in this book may have changed since publication and may no longer be valid. The views expressed in this work are solely those of the author and do not necessarily reflect the views of the publisher, and the publisher hereby disclaims any responsibility for them.

Any people depicted in stock imagery provided by Thinkstock are models, and such images are being used for illustrative purposes only.

Certain stock imagery © Thinkstock.

ISBN: 978-1-4624-0291-5 (sc)
ISBN: 978-1-4624-0292-2 (e)

Library of Congress Control Number: 2012915115

Printed in the United States of America

Inspiring Voices rev. date: 08/28/2012

# Contents

No Dark Peace. . . . . . . . . . . . . 1
A World Someday . . . . . . . . . . 2
Danny's Lost. . . . . . . . . . . . . . 3
Don't Quit . . . . . . . . . . . . . . . 4
Nowhere Usa . . . . . . . . . . . . . 5
Tranquill. . . . . . . . . . . . . . . . 6
Only One Home . . . . . . . . . . 7
Taking Credit Gaining Power . . . . . 8
Hopefully Talking . . . . . . . . . . 9
Not A Winner . . . . . . . . . . . 10
Just Know Why . . . . . . . . . . 11
A Love . . . . . . . . . . . . . . . . 12
No Lines . . . . . . . . . . . . . . . 13
No Job . . . . . . . . . . . . . . . . 14
To Sing . . . . . . . . . . . . . . . 15
Children Grow. . . . . . . . . . . . 16
Just Believe. . . . . . . . . . . . . 17
Same Mistakes. . . . . . . . . . . 18
Just Caring. . . . . . . . . . . . . . 19
We All Need Help . . . . . . . . . 20
Time To Stop . . . . . . . . . . . 21
No Money Needed . . . . . . . . 22
Give More . . . . . . . . . . . . . 23
Trying To Quit . . . . . . . . . . . 24
They Haunt . . . . . . . . . . . . 25
Just Truth . . . . . . . . . . . . . 26
Overcome . . . . . . . . . . . . . 27
Talking To Loud. . . . . . . . . . 28

| | |
|---|---|
| Forgive Those | 29 |
| Too Little | 30 |
| Awaken | 31 |
| To Be Timid | 32 |
| Natures Kisses | 33 |
| Forgive A Few For So Many | 34 |
| Why Stop A Life | 35 |
| The March | 36 |
| Keep Trying | 37 |
| The Jealous | 38 |
| To Moody | 39 |
| The Dating Game | 40 |
| With Payment | 41 |
| What's A Choice | 42 |
| To Many Ideas | 43 |
| A Happy Day | 44 |
| Can't Be Recognized | 45 |
| No Plan For Home | 46 |
| In Our Mind | 47 |
| Our Feelings | 48 |
| Let Me Forget | 49 |
| Overcome Just Overcome | 50 |
| Wrong Information | 51 |
| Thier Own Thing | 52 |
| The Top Bouncer | 53 |
| Try To Give | 54 |
| Don't Let This Night End | 55 |
| Western Challenge | 56 |
| A Little To Often | 57 |
| Too Sexual | 58 |
| As Children Grow | 59 |
| Crime Failure | 60 |
| High School Truths | 61 |
| No Hope | 62 |

| | |
|---|---|
| Too Few | 63 |
| Hopefully Over | 64 |
| What Is True | 65 |
| A Peaceful Field | 66 |
| She's Mine | 67 |
| Treasure Time | 68 |
| Think Of Truth | 69 |
| What Kind Of Relationship | 70 |
| Dedication | 71 |
| No Surprises | 72 |
| When You're Right | 73 |
| Ones Choice | 74 |
| Worrying | 75 |
| Coming Of Wisdom | 76 |
| Take The Chance | 77 |
| Failure In Sight | 78 |
| Disturbing | 79 |
| Someone Proud | 80 |
| Somethings Senseless | 81 |
| A Days Toils | 82 |
| Flying By | 83 |
| It Can Happen | 84 |
| A Civil End | 85 |
| Make Life Happen | 86 |
| The Lost Life | 87 |
| To Cherish | 88 |
| Giving | 89 |
| Growing Together | 90 |
| Part Of Me | 91 |
| A Natures Strength | 92 |
| The Room | 93 |
| Carry On | 94 |
| To Visit Woonsocket | 95 |
| Growing Together | 96 |

| | |
|---|---|
| Nowhere Usa | 97 |
| No End Of Taking | 98 |
| Why Has Life | 99 |
| Always Running | 100 |
| A Readers Prize | 101 |
| Lost Ones Way | 102 |
| Reaching Goals | 103 |
| So Many Times | 104 |
| Without Guidance | 105 |
| Be Careful | 106 |
| A Treat | 107 |
| Who's To Decide | 108 |
| The Songs Of Nature | 109 |
| Those Controlled | 110 |
| Time Goes On | 111 |
| No Church | 112 |
| This Man | 113 |
| How Could Some | 114 |
| A Childs Determination | 115 |
| Overcoming | 116 |
| To Loose Everything | 117 |
| Why So Many | 118 |
| In Oneself | 119 |
| A Portrait Victim | 120 |
| May Someone Save | 121 |
| No Dates | 122 |
| Boulder Girls | 123 |
| Too Many Years | 124 |
| Selfishly | 125 |
| Which Decision | 126 |
| Why The Failure | 127 |
| To Comment | 128 |
| A Path Of Learning | 129 |
| Cnog | 130 |

So Many Truths . . . . . . . . . . . 131
Growing At A Lost . . . . . . . . 132
Cnog The Beginning . . . . . . . 133
A Psychological Battle . . . . . . . 134
No More . . . . . . . . . . . . . . 135
The Jibberish . . . . . . . . . 136
No More, The Weapon . . . . . . 137
No Where To Live . . . . . . . . . 138
Will The Clock Stop . . . . . . . . 139
A Police Letdown . . . . . . . . . 140
A Better Life . . . . . . . . . . . . 141
The Mistakes . . . . . . . . . . 142
Weapons Of Peace . . . . . . . . 143
For The Proud Girl . . . . . . . . 144
A Movement Lost . . . . . . . . . 145
Soldier . . . . . . . . . . . . . . . 146
A Torn Mind . . . . . . . . . . . 147
So Many Men . . . . . . . . . . 148
Probably Unhappy . . . . . . . . 149
A Day Or Two . . . . . . . . . . . 150
A Chapel . . . . . . . . . . . . . . 151
The Lonely Job . . . . . . . . . . 152
A Buisness Calamity . . . . . . . . 153
Forget Nyc . . . . . . . . . . . . . 154
Civil Obediance . . . . . . . . . . 155
An Open Heart . . . . . . . . . . 156
The Prisoner . . . . . . . . . . . . 157
State Mental Institution . . . . . . 158
A Few Books . . . . . . . . . . . . 159
Trapped . . . . . . . . . . . . . . 160
Close The Bar . . . . . . . . . . . 161
To Many Children . . . . . . . . . 162
No Clouds . . . . . . . . . . . . . 163
The Draft . . . . . . . . . . . . . 164

The Jounalist. . . . . . . . . . . . . .165
Life Goes On  . . . . . . . . . . . .166
Don't Cry . . . . . . . . . . . . . .167
There Is So Many . . . . . . . . . .168
Traveling Thoughts . . . . . . . . .169
Wonderful Feelings  . . . . . . . . .170
Understanding Ones-Self . . . . . .171
Survival Skills . . . . . . . . . . . .172
Givng Up . . . . . . . . . . . . . .173
Don't Give Up. . . . . . . . . . . .174
The End . . . . . . . . . . . . . . .175
To Be Recognized . . . . . . . . . .176
Can't Hold. . . . . . . . . . . . . .177
The Price Of Communicating . . .178
The Math Is Wrong . . . . . . . . .179
To Conquer The Elements . . . . .180
Till When . . . . . . . . . . . . . .181
Second Best . . . . . . . . . . . . .182
The Cost . . . . . . . . . . . . . . .183
The Report  . . . . . . . . . . . . .184
To Pass On. . . . . . . . . . . . . .185
Pray For Life . . . . . . . . . . . . .186
Some May Be  . . . . . . . . . . . .187
Awarded . . . . . . . . . . . . . . .188
No Challenge  . . . . . . . . . . . .189
Home Life . . . . . . . . . . . . . .190
Cnog. . . . . . . . . . . . . . . . .191
Impossible To Lead . . . . . . . . .192
Rhode Island  . . . . . . . . . . . .193
In Just Thought . . . . . . . . . . .194
Many Events. . . . . . . . . . . . .195
We're All Chosen  . . . . . . . . . .196
A New Beginning . . . . . . . . . .197
Press On . . . . . . . . . . . . . . .198

At Peace . . . . . . . . . . . . . . . . .199
Learning To Much . . . . . . . . .200
Dangerous Tack . . . . . . . . . . . .201
One To Powerful . . . . . . . . . .202
All Can Overcome. . . . . . . . . .203
Not To Brave . . . . . . . . . . . . .204
Mistaken . . . . . . . . . . . . . . . .205
In Touch With Oneself . . . . . . .206
Finding Nature . . . . . . . . . . . .207
Wherever It Happens . . . . . . . .208
Always Alone . . . . . . . . . . . .209
Good Morning . . . . . . . . . . .210
Scared . . . . . . . . . . . . . . . . .211
Someone Cares . . . . . . . . . . .212
Raising . . . . . . . . . . . . . . . . .213
Life's Toils . . . . . . . . . . . . . .214
A Life . . . . . . . . . . . . . . . . .215
A Long Time . . . . . . . . . . . .216
Senses . . . . . . . . . . . . . . . . .217
Waiting For A Change . . . . . . .218
Witness . . . . . . . . . . . . . . . .219
Anyone Can . . . . . . . . . . . . .220

# No Dark Peace

its night
and all the fight
is put to rest
because at its best
it must grow
because
it's time to go
and find
the right kind
at this time

# A World Someday

money
can't buy peace
with weapons
that leaves
us
without
our lives
and need
of environment
where money
can't barter
us peace

# Danny's Lost

so tired
so wronged
and at last
a joke
until the truth
which will flow
in the time
they will see
the lies
and peace
will settle
in ones heart

# Don't Quit

tired
of being tired
broken
in spirit
and with
all the rest
we still
are missing
the dreams
at night
and the will
to forget

# Nowhere USA

it's cold in the middle
of summer
and rains
almost always
there is no warmth
around people
who don't care
but for whom
it's advantageous
to flatter
and lead on

# Tranquill

the chill of the night
lightens her up
as the days drag
the night
presents itself
on a flight
of peace

# Only One Home

a list
of knots
no lists
for progress
because the lists
got buried
with the trash
and only though
recycling
an endeavor
worth the time
to find the lost

# Taking Credit Gaining Power

    the prime benefactors
    of indiscretion
    need not
    be heard
    they have lost
    the dream
    which we all
    hold so dear

# Hopefully Talking

on call
with no phone
yet
one can hear
the ringing
that only comes
at certain times
and
it won't stop
because without
the phone
it can't
be answered
without someone
on the other end

# Not A Winner

    we lost
    not a race
    to be
    not a contest
    to be
    we lost the test
    of a hopeful time
    we lost
    it will be

# Just Know Why

a clean break
from the past
of the heart
or the solitude
of life
means
we need not run
and hide
to be proud

# A Love

the many gods
of the many cultures
over
the millenniums
have varied
and often came
as fast as they
left
is our god
our lord
hopefully

# No Lines

a single word
with several meanings
to few
for the many
who seek
the meaning
or the ways
to observe
words
in motion

# No Job

a few dollars
come
from so far away
no personal
interaction
except
a banker
whose pockets
are deep

# To Sing

all along
we knew all to well
there would be no song
but as time will tell
we sing
of love
and it will bring
us above
the prey
and we will fight
as the brave
with all our might

# Children Grow

the flip top
is the start
of a journey
where we've
been before
but choose to return
over and over
again
there comes a time
we must say
to the flip top
and the horror
it can bring

# Just Believe

if we can love
ourselves
with never ending
faith
we receive love
from God
who loves us
whatever
our failings

# Same Mistakes

lost in the time
of our lives
where we are vulnerable
to life's trials
for some
it's when they are young
but the few
who can't grow up
they live
life
as a revolving door
over and over

# Just Caring

a friend
indeed
doesn't need
a vision
of himself
true or false
but accept
those
who
befriend him

# We All Need Help

the change
in our pockets
can help change
the lives
of those
who can't help
themselves
but it takes
many pockets
to buy
hope

# Time To Stop

with one foot
near the grave
would we have the sense
to
change our habits
while we still
have one foot
on solid ground
or do we
have the will
to face
tomorrows challenges
in today's world

# No Money Needed

in all the world
there are heroes
past and present
but the price
they pay
makes no cents
like money
love and honor
can't be bought
but destroyed
in the search
of those
who make no sense

# Give More

a gift
from God
is for all
who wish
to receive
and
to bring joy
to our young
who grasp
the meaning
of love
with all its
gifts

# Trying To Quit

the last puff
will never be enough
there is always
one more
and
one more
will it end
or
will it end me

# They Haunt

a single thought
of a single man
left alone
with growth
of the heart
yet the thoughts
come more often
and not only
a single man
but disillusioned

# Just Truth

indeed
our society
have those
who wish
to impress
not just others
but can with hold
their feelings
as a person
past and present

# Overcome

a moment
of silence
meditation
in a prayer
tired from
the early morn
the start
of the day
and the pain
will perish
into the night

# Talking To Loud

a brisk walk
with a lot
of talk
there's no reset
just play
it just stay
the talk
along the walk

# Forgive Those

I don't know
if I know
I wouldn't
want to know
are feelings
so sensitive
that pain
can be inflicted
by a few choice words
I don't know
only if I knew

# Too Little

at a devastating cost
the dollar
was stretched
until it tore
now again
another dollar
must take its place
again
at what cost

# Awaken

all along
time
stood still
the alarm
went off
and seconds
added up
to minutes
of change

# To Be Timid

the cold
on an environmental
holding pattern
it comes
it conquers
and leaves
in peace

# Natures Kisses

the chill
in the air
the winds
whirl
the snow
along the ground
there is a movement
of serenity
on the land

# Forgive A Few For So Many

if they know
how it feels
they wouldn't care
nothing would change
yet
to protect others
the game
may never end
but go from
field to field
never filling
a stadium

# Why Stop A Life

all along
they knew
but wouldn't
admit
what would change
the devastation
of a mind
that needs rest
of to head
for the future

# The March

a short foot
can't exit
a yard doesn't
measure
what marches
left and right
need be
consistent
in a group
so there may be
a long foot

# Keep Trying

a grand vision
blind to indecision
battled with little slack
forever attempting a comeback
as if we didn't know
but we must grasp
a little bit of the past

# The Jealous

    stalled
    with
    the motor running
    Non-stop adventure
    quietly
    with self evidence
    the motor
    will stall
    left to death

# To Moody

the dark side
hides
feeling the most
the light side
reflects the tide
but the ocean
can't be harnessed
with the tides
ever changing

# THE DATING GAME

short on time
long on patience
with little
persistence
some can be conquered
while others pass
depending
on which second
the clack stops

# With Payment

a host of options
some charged
some cash
none to be bought
none to be sold
sometimes
possession
is only a dream

# What's A Choice

bitten
and chewed
a decision
to be made
while simultaneously
trying to live
within one body
taken from the heart
left challenged
and distorted
until unrecognizable

# To Many Ideas

it happens
with or without
approval
opinions come
opinions go
it happens
sometime for the best
sometimes for the worst
but it happens

# A Happy Day

live with
live without
but live
a life
of pride
and dignity
for ones own
self esteem
can't be
left home
or
stored away

# Can't Be Recognized

the long
the short
it may even
be a dress
a raincoat
to disguise
the short
of the long

# No Plan For Home

off the back
to
a new front
for what's to come
if it came before
it hasn't changed
but time has
but not enough

# In Our Mind

interwinded
thoughts
without purpose
can be left
indescribable
to many
who need
so much
who have been
given so little
with only hope

# Our Feelings

crystal
can shine
under light
but
in darkness
it is just glass
as breakable
as it may be

# Let Me Forget

a figure
in public
disguised
with a mask
to hide the spirit
of whom
so much
has meant
so little
for so long
with little hope

# Overcome Just Overcome

a broken arm
in a cast
maybe a weapon
for who knows
a hopeless feeling
but other
than those
whose handicaps
won't let
freedom prevail

# Wrong Information

gagging
choking
wallowing
could very well
be a message
that the beckoning
for the cause
can't be swallowed

# Thier Own Thing

going, going
left
with the truth
left undiscovered
why people
don't understand
because
there's
no reason to

# The Top Bouncer

a staff
of fools
without a clue
control the night
and hidden
in the darkness
is the truth
without light
remains
the rules
of the players
for
their own sake

# Try To Give

lift
your heart
with
a little patience
a little understanding
but lift
for all among us
regardless
of those
who are heartless

# Don't Let This Night End

congratulations
in the moon light
won't stop
the sun from arriving
it may
be just
a gesture
of peacefulness

# Western Challenge

lassoes
tide to the post
break away
with one gust
blown off track
in a struggle
to succeed

# A Little To Often

so forbidden
with some remorse
a claim of grievance
was all but lost
and something strange
came to the source
the truth
a road across
to dignity
so all
is not lost

# Too Sexual

loosely fit
for cover
of which
is part
of a drive
for the sake
of the few
who care

# As Children Grow

a gift
from God
should be
for God
if not for whom
would seek the reward
for so little
for so long

# CRIME FAILURE

all alone
on a journey
with no reward
so much
effort
needed
for so little
and if
it works

# High School Truths

because
for whom
it was
a deed
without regret
for those
who held
the truth
were not asked
why
is forgiveness
granted

# No Hope

discarded without regard

without a home
what else
none in charge
what else
as low
as low as possible
what else
no end in sight
may God bless

## Too Few

give till it hurts
and give a little more
stop for the pain
of those who disdain
they are not
chosen
to compare
the dear not dare
to feel
and care

# Hopefully Over

all I care
is with a stare
little imagination
is left over
for those who dare
there is no stare
self confident
aside
good-bye

# What Is True

in time
all's fine
at the place
in the window
if the window
cracks
all that's fine
is distorted
with a believing
setting

# A Peaceful Field

pieces of gold
sprinkled in the pasture
sunlight glistening
beauty
not to be forgotten
none
can conquer it
just treasure
it as a treasure

# She's Mine

pearls and orchids
as pure
as fleece
gathered as presents
presents for someone
someone
who is special
special to some
unknown
to most

# Treasure Time

cost of life
may
have no limits
but
a happy life
need not
have a price tag
it may
be worth it
to frown
but being happy
is a virtue

# Think Of Truth

gruesome thoughts
can delete
the soul
kind thoughts
can bring about
a smile
causing disillusionment
is a liars game
coming
by the truth
is the beginning

# What Kind Of Relationship

can a diamond
gain meaning
is love
a commodity
is talk cheap
or
the conquer
of loneliness
is set
for sale
or does sharing
have meaning

# Dedication

a calling
can lead
to self-destruction
a ministry
can be condemned
wander forever
is seldom good
good thing's
come
in unknown packages

# No Surprises

gosh it can't
get worse
looking
for a change
for the better
not a lot
to overcome
just don't
come up empty

# When You're Right

acceptance
through perseverance
defaulted
on false accusations
claims adjusted
to for go
the truth
what's wrong
can hurt
what's right
stands alone

# Ones Choice

loosing the battle
to believe
views come
from many angles
you can only hope
to find answers
but you must
be willing
to believe

# Worrying

breezes at night
rain all day
chills
in the spine
sweat
on the forehead
worrying endlessly
for no reason

# Coming Of Wisdom

found
in the dark
groomed
in the daylight
beauty
holds many secrets
not the secret
of youth
but
coming of age
to bloom
will enrich
our society

# Take The Chance

opportunities created
is goals achieved
falling
by the wayside
is a fruitless
endeavor
grab the moment
live life
with meaning

# Failure In Sight

a default
unlucky
can and does
comes the
worst times
obstacles
often
in the way
climbing higher
means you can
fall further

# Disturbing

cause for disdain
and thinning patience
holding in forever
mumbling
not happy
what reasons
are worth this
a lot
if you try
to understand

# Someone Proud

a distance
from further
closing the gap
efforts made
effort paying off
love, like or friend
dad is there
the most

# Somethings Senseless

tossed aside
and laughed at
humoring society
made fun of
jokes, jokes, jokes
many girls
can outgrow
however
and how
and why
grow up
to be
laughed at
again

# A Days Toils

coming down
from a haze
gently arising
from slumber
sunshine and peace
why must we change
turmoil and distrust
forgetting a friend
must we stop
and wonder

# Flying By

    it takes
    it tolls
    be money
    or stress
    choosing
    with a vengeance
    with all the help
    working
    there is no more me
    to talk to

# It Can Happen

good luck
bad luck
no luck
it's often about
patience
and the work
leading
in the direction
the direction
of love

# A Civil End

all the time
of the fad
all the areas
considered alright
might be the end
of notions
long held
but if not a fad
are things
really
any different

# Make Life Happen

living on less can straighten out a mess
caused over
a long time
can you hear that song
time comes to change
life needs to be rearranged
It's all a bet
with many regrets

# The Lost Life

were always last
because of our past
can't get a job
living like a slob
won't over turn
without a change
and come to grasp
we've already lost

# To Cherish

touched
by an enchanted spirit
full of love
and understanding
often
so often
things end in tragedy
let us be thankful
for what little we have

# Giving

living
oh so much
taken for granted
we have our health
we can live
productively
and giving
to those
who hurt

# Growing Together

with a child
one becomes a parent
what child
need not two parents
a calling
of experience
to bring to the world
a child who ourselves
are proud

# Part Of Me

the limit
on limits
is no where
in sight
time comes
time goes
but life
stops
momentarily
so suffering
is imminent
in my life

# A Natures Strength

a seed
can grow to a tree
some may bear fruit
some are just shade
but in all
we have been given
a pacifier
to cherish

# The Room

with the quiet
a break of
the silence
squalls
throughout the room
almost
a jail
with no sentence
but life
It's conquered
by
disillusionment

# Carry On

my God
who I don't understand
my God
who lets me live
my God
who can conquer
my God
give
me the strength

# To Visit Woonsocket

three hours
to travel
to unknown
with little
help
from
anyone
who may
just as well be
everyone
time hasn't healed
the wounds
will anything
be all right

# GROWING TOGETHER

with a child
one becomes a parent
what child
need not two parents
a calling
of experience
to bring to the world
a child who ourselves
are proud

# Nowhere USA

it's cold in the middle
of summer
and rains
almost always
there is no warmth
around people
who don't care
but for whom
it's advantageous
to flatter
and lead on

# No End Of Taking

my, my
we all
want a piece
of the pie
of the pie
we wish not
to be the cooker
we all wish
for a slice
to enrich
ourselves

# Why Has Life

were we born
to be happy
were we born
to fail
how was
lives
moments
planned out
and were there
mistakes
that can't
be amended

# Always Running

bye-bye
never say goodbye
bye-bye
can we light
up the sky
bye-bye
be never
meant to leave
bye-bye
its
the best

# A Readers Prize

sale a paper
a nickel
a dime
or two
but without doubt
quite a few
a reward
no
move forward
for two

# Lost Ones Way

    thrown out as wrote
    uncleansable over years
    talking of a lifetime
    in and out
    of supplies
    destined
    to spurn society
    way are some
    in such disarrays

# Reaching Goals

like it a lot
not a little
like it a lot
measures can be taken
to secure
what one has
but none should
be of a person
who would take it away
for those people
have the problem

# So Many Times

if we can weep
from happiness
can we cry
in sorrow
or when
we are
helpless
in a world
around us
and told
to be silent
can we just weep

# Without Guidance

only a little bit
of luck
from time to time
can define
a lives path
so little
at a time
so we must
keep hope

# Be Careful

chew a bite
but don't be bitten
catch a fish
but don't
turn up in the net
don't watch the pot boil
because at times
it is inevitable
as a person
the temper
boils

# A Treat

loosen the belt
rattle the change
in for a treat
this time
maybe really neat
don't rush
be patient
life is precious

# Who's To Decide

I like myself
I don't like myself
I don't want myself
but if change
is inevitable
I want to run
run, run, run
until I like
myself

# The Songs Of Nature

listen to the song
it's a birds love
life is neutral
but not
behind walls
a natural gift
but are
we as people
are worthy

# Those Controlled

why not
if someone objects
is there a reason
or an excuse
that the will
of many
be controlled
by one
one hundred
one thousand
may be
in a free society
it's to disagree

# Time Goes On

mistakes of youth
can be forgotten
but
an insensitive
judgement
or society
that values
the past
can't recognize
the future

# No Church

a little effort
with no heart
driven
to be decisive
can break
the backs
of the lonely
or tormented
serving
God

# This Man

at
what cost
is
the prestige
of an individual
that
he be
above
what is right
in the eyes
of those
who be
blind
to the truth

# How Could Some

the feelings
to travel
to protest
the young
is overpowering
but what good
can come
from the humiliation
of those
so innocent
who strive
for a better
life

# A Childs Determination

when
never to tired
to care
then
the energy
in what sparkles
in the eyes
of those
to young
to lust
for life's
unforgiveness

# Overcoming

growing stronger everyday
becoming a found man
in come the responsibility
out
goes the found man
one more time
maybe
two more times

# To Loose Everything

as we grew
together
the change
was significant
I just got
old
and maybe
with no future
there is nothing
to loose
but
a small change

# Why So Many

even things
so miniscule
can't be distorted
and enlarged
to suit
the amusement
of those
who anguish
in
the self denial
of spite

# In Oneself

the anger
comes
sometimes
very often
the alcohol
could
control only
so much
left dry
we may not
be thirsty
but
we could explode

# A Portrait Victim

who
can here
the thoughts
cast
by the lonely
in
an effort
to alter
a persecution
created
by those
who choose
to cause disappear

# May Someone Save

listless and fearful
crying for understanding
who will try
to listen
will the sun shine
will tomorrow
bring change

# No Dates

we can give
until
all we have
is gone
and to find
the hope
to revive
our relationships
the time
will pass by
with a vengeance
without
love

# Boulder Girls

while
so young
and innocent
and attempting
to change
the generation
they call their own
they deserve
the respect
and admiration
and even
and encouraging word
from those
who care

# Too Many Years

living a life
that requires
the passage
of time
takes
the patience
to endure
and
the fortitude
to understand
people often
see the light
even
when it's dark

# Selfishly

wasting so much
to feel sorry
for oneself
defeating help
causing
so much pain
with little effort
so much
could have meaning

# Which Decision

we can go
in many directions
even some
in the past
to build
a new future
with all
its flair
it will take
a consensus
of the young
for they alone
hold the key
to
their future

# Why The Failure

when we loose
our youthful
sense of direction
purpose
becomes embroiled
by expectations
of a society
in which
if you don't
succeed
You're lastly
looked upon
as a failure

# To Comment

they told us
and
what they said
wasn't true
but what
they said
changed
which
Were the lies
of those
who
most of all
need
to tell
the truth

# A Path Of Learning

for my trouble
I've come nowhere
I've seen
so much
felt such feelings
done so little
for so many
may someday
I'll just understand

# Cnog

we arose
surrounded
by the controversy
of a generation
who gave us life
and the insights
of life itself
or what
it could be
and
it could change
for better
and better

# So Many Truths

in our heart
we hold
the feelings
we can't
let out
because
we must be
a part
of society
where
honestly
doesn't matter

# Growing At A Lost

we arose
from
are destinies
as with
we could change
not
the unchangeable
but what
life was
to be
later in life
with confidence

# Cnog The Beginning

born upon
a spring night
and those
who choose
while young
and inexperienced
in the ways
of life
can light
a torch
which only
I could destroy
over and over
again

# A Psychological Battle

in the model
of those
left uninformed
because
within the mind
there
is a difference
of order
and operation
which
makes life's pleasures
difficult

# No More

the spark
is gone
in times
of trouble
which
is prolonged
by the darkness
brought
upon
the inner self
where pride
becomes
a thing
of the past

# The Jibberish

    coast to coast
    the boast
    is to be
    the toast
    with little regard
    how far
    one must go
    to know
    it doesn't matter
    because
    in the latter
    the proof
    is the truth

# No More, The Weapon

to listen
to the words
is the concentration
of communication
when the words
stumble
in ways
that many
may tell
that one
may not have
the abilities
to succeed
on their own

# No Where To Live

our lives
are short
but
long enough
to feel pain
anger and sorrow
and the regrets
of our mistakes
but we need
to seek happiness
in whatever place
we can call
home

# Will The Clock Stop

if time
stands still
it is patience
a clock
can't remit
but time
will always
continue
and time
need not
be an enemy
but can be
an ally

# A Police Letdown

        they deliver
        in most cases
        but can't
        by themselves
        secure
        our freedoms
        by themselves
        because
        at times
        for those
        who care
        can't get an audience
        for what
        they feel
        either

# A Better Life

in a world
where homes
out price
the people
who have
not the resources
to cohabitant
as a family
the children
look
for the
leadership within
to transform
a market

# The Mistakes

loosing the grasp
of destiny
controlling
ones attitude
indifferent
to what's best
coming on strong
something
is happening
as things crumble
a lot
is learned

# Weapons Of Peace

slashing out words
meaningless
while angry
just as lightning crackles
and thunder
breaks the silence
doom is predicted
but the gates
of the future
are open
and with it
happiness

# For The Proud Girl

an easy way out
is no way
to get in
get in
deep
with penetrating thoughts
with
no cash value
to anyone

# A Movement Lost

hostile
improbable
impossible
but they're lying
is the foundation
to be built upon
on and on
until we built
the unbuildable

# Soldier

the babe
that chilled
the shoulders
of the soldier
in the army
gave orders
but the babes
who chill
the soldiers
come and go
but
so many
are left alone

# A Torn Mind

all the excitement
with little fanfare
going
after goals
dismissed by the press
pressure
grows
but
there is no steam
coming from
the pressure cooker
inside

# So Many Men

a cause
to fight for
in worth
may be infamous
to those
with the key
the key
the key
to unlock
the chains
which hold us
separate
and apart
of the mainstream

# Probably Unhappy

to punish
to deceive
to ridicule
is in people
who've lost
their path
and have chosen a road
which will not
lead to happiness

# A Day Or Two

a holiday
a time for cheer
and time off
or
is it time
to replenish
old furnaces
which continue
to burn
year round

# A Chapel

when the bells ring
to light the path
with sounds
from within
and to search for more
but give thanks
for all
we have

# The Lonely Job

we can't start
a new life
like
starting a new job
because
for some
it's too hard
to find
our qualities
marketable
since often
we can't
give of ourselves

# A Buisness Calamity

to cute
to be a fool
but a tool
of those
who knew
they'd get caught
it was
only
a clause
in the contract

# Forget Nyc

if I felt
pressure
to succumb to
adversity
to which
was silly
I would walk
and walk
and
never look back

# Civil Obediance

why
the strange
things
that happen
always
happen
to us
and we seem
to accept
the role
of victims

# An Open Heart

we can't
console
the victims
who
may not
live to a tune
of vengeance
but
forgiveness

# The Prisoner

when
we're all alone
there's a sense
that our minds
might
drift
in directions
independent
of the feelings
they touch
or the
torture
they cause

# STATE MENTAL INSTITUTION

when all is gone
what may be left
may not
be worth saving
the death
of a shell
of a person
belongs
in God's hands
not for individual
pity

# A Few Books

life begins
with knowledge
and until
time comes
where what's
inside
matters
the knowledge
becomes outdated
because
of age
as time passes quickly

# Trapped

the tears
wash away
the trauma
but can't
recycle
a mind
congested
with
the experience
that lives
on and on
as if
in a prison

# Close The Bar

the closure
of what's right
belongs
to those
Whose life
passes the test
for the well being
of most
but not all

# To Many Children

all the cash
one
may need
will vary
with time
forever
a burden
that's life's
presents
particularly
for those
with
to little
and forgotten

# No Clouds

we can't
live our lives
like the wind
blowing
at times endlessly
at times calm
we need
a constant breeze
to live in peace
and harmony

# The Draft

it may be
a tied score
but it doesn't
mean
the players are equal
it just allows
a team or teams
to determine
the outcome
of a player
or players

# THE JOUNALIST

I can't tell
while
walking among
the people
who believe
it is
in their names
that print
shall revolve
a tittle
claimed
by pleasure

# Life Goes On

all in all
life goes on
at a crawl
or a gallop
sometimes
our heads spin
sometimes
out of control
but
to retreat
would
be the end
of the beginning

## Don't Cry

don't cry
it won't help
the hurt
will hurt
without regard
for those
who care
the hurt
will always
be there
as we drive
ourselves
for all eternity
which
is now

# There Is So Many

the holidays
that brings
happiness
to so many
happens
to be solemn
for others
when we dream
we should dream
for all

# Traveling Thoughts

groveling a thought
reaching for a solution
one problem
after another
holding moments apart
got to keep in pace
stepping to time
but walking slowly

# Wonderful Feelings

to catch
the glow
among
the Christians
and women
to bear children
and the gifts
for those
who receive
can't be judged
or
conquered

# Understanding Ones-Self

failing without effort
coming to terms
with ones-self
goals forever blocked
taking a step back
coming to terms
someday leading
a productive life

# Survival Skills

with peace
in the heart
things
fall in place
for those
whose paths
lead them
not in adventure
but
of the need
of survival skills
for life

# Givng Up

to slow
to stay
in the flow
because
of the pay
and if
it comes
to
dollars and cents
it
makes no sense
to stay
in the flow
for many

# Don't Give Up

if we
must die
is it before
our best works
are
to come
or
are we permanently
burnt
on both ends
to see
ourselves
through

# The End

a hole
in the head
may hold
the relief
of the suffering
for those
who have
so little
it may come
in the form
of a bullet
instead
of a blow
that can heal

# To Be Recognized

with the promotion
on the line
will one
look
the wrong way
when things
are going
his way
or will he
rock the boat
and earn
the recognition
and defeat

# Can't Hold

I can't hold
in my heart
for the duration
of life
most likely
shorter
than
longer
but
to the grave
there will be
no time
to let go

# The Price Of Communicating

when most
are mislead
by the communication
of public ideas
and yet gain
the advantage
financially
and the power
is not to be
mistaken
but
is untrustworthy

# The Math Is Wrong

it all adds up
it all the zeros
are
correctly placed
but
the math
is the score
of disappointment
and being wrong
is hurtful

# To Conquer The Elements

it damp
and chilly
but we must
make this
our moments
if we can
overcome
nature
we'll be able
to compete
whether
its
warm
or
cold

# Till When

in a hurry
to get
the flurry
of thoughts
and
ever present ideas
out of
the prison
in my mind
and
undo paper
where
they wait
till when
they are discovered

# Second Best

trying
to be
the best
is not
the only thing
some
should strive
for
second best
but
it doesn't matter
for those
who try
can find
a niche

# The Cost

you can't play
your best
if you don't
pay
the price
of the prize
and paying
brings
only a few
the awards

# The Report

with any news
good or bad
the style
of the report
can make
or break
the innocent
or the perpetrator
usually ends
with one
worst
or better

# To Pass On

if we could
tell anyone
who may listen
a tale
of woes
and
then move on
just knowing
we won't die
in vain

# Pray For Life

in death
of we can
see a solution
which
were looking at
the wrong problem
may decide
our fate
life or death
and
only in pray
can life
become
tolerable

# Some May Be

some may be
just a little
wishy washy
a kind
of person
who temporarily
was
hung out
to dry
with
the dirty laundry

# Awarded

should we grasp
at the awards
that brings us
nowhere
with such praise
which brings
a persistent
end to a journey
which
may be
just the beginning

# No Challenge

the education
of which
is deemed
acceptable
may not
have the quality
of home
for thought

# Home Life

all the apprehension
for an award
not forth coming
and the need
to share
the heartbreak
of a cycle
in two decades
of somber
harassment
and
trauma

# Cnog

along the roads
of destiny
are the stops
to rest
and to regain
the hope
that began
a long time ago

# Impossible To Lead

the correct
obviously
are faulted
when wrong
and not
encouraged
when right
but left
to be controlled
not by wisdom
but default

# Rhode Island

when it's cold
and there
is no warmth
It's then
we wander
until
we are just
so tired
that
our last search
is a place
to sleep
hopefully
a church

# In Just Thought

slowly
time moves
without
a pause
but many
have the time
to get lost
in thought
and time
seems
to pass by

# Many Events

we gather
to pay homage
at many events
that may
not have occurred
if things
had been different
and time
presented occasions
that could
be seen
it would be
through
most eyes

# We're All Chosen

the lost crown
of the child
was soiled
by the earth
could a new bearer
overcome disillusionment
or was the soul
tainted and unforgiving
but
a fathers bequest
came to life

# A New Beginning

a young man
grappled with his feelings
but a nation lost
can only
have a beginning

# Press On

the snakes venom
sullened the prophet
soon only
warnings came forth
could he still
be held
as the one to fulfill
or was he
overcome
by a bondage
with truth

# At Peace

along the road
was a ditch
beholden
in the ditch
was moisture
could I now
understand
how a cloud
can nurture nature
and hence
is at peace
with its self

# Learning To Much

fall, fall, falling
not downward
but in a spiral
not up
or down
but
in solemn truth
truth
that came
the hard way

# Dangerous Tack

the solemn truth
is the only word
in many ways
words change
what is first
seldom comes last
what comes last
can often
haunt

# One To Powerful

if one
can change destiny
then only time
can heal
what
is to come forth
and change
can only come
when destiny
groups
what it must

# All Can Overcome

if someone lost
can kick in
the willpower
do terms have
to be decided
by fate
fate need not
be a part of destiny
overcoming
destiny
is in ourselves

# Not To Brave

is strength
really as strong
as if
you could see
what you saw
can might
overcome fear
if the fear
is dealt with
not why
how come

# Mistaken

worst then before
is realizing after
not knowing
can be wonderful
but when
it's there
it is
to be believed

# In Touch With Oneself

I can feel something
I know its real
I know it has depth
finding it
may be an adventure
but
there can be something
wonderful in a feeling

# Finding Nature

the solemn
unspoken word
of the wind
speaking softly
and
bringing us to rest
man will inevitably
stir up a conversation
lets make sure
it's the right one

# Wherever It Happens

walking softly
through the field
holding the silence dear
a crow speaks out
he may be looking
for a friend
a friend
he may have found

# Always Alone

I've seen the sun
but the darkness
is blinding
even voices
become mumbled
and thoughts
become distorted
with these sensations
time has come
to find
a friend

# Good Morning

dear misses sunshine
I'm feeling blue
with the summertime blues
let the day
start right
with a tic toc
and only
time will tell

# Scared

will those left
without harmony
of fellowship
grasp meaning
less thinking
of me is
left alone
and becoming fierce
only chilled
without emotion
never to gather
together

# Someone Cares

calling out
but no one will listen
crying with no one
to wipe the tears
alone and lost
drawn back
and hoping
to reach out
and being touched

# Raising

nurture the children
to grow
and to dream
be slow to judge
and long on patience
overcome imagery
and love will surface
when it comes time for advice
don't be within yourself

# Life's Toils

long lost feelings
why did they leave
hardened by cruelty
without feelings
or emotions
coming to grasp reality
with no hiding places
left
it won't end
because it's just
the beginning

# A Life

I'll find it
I lost it
it's somewhere
but not here
gone now
gone later
it may
be worth finding
but I had
it all along

# A Long Time

lowing grin
confused and threatened
time to stop
help has to arrive
as time slows
light begins to shine
when it's over
it may never end

# Senses

causes for alarm
sound we can't hear
depending on senses
darkness in the corner
learning to cope
coping for life

# Waiting For A Change

waiting for a chance
held back by intolerance
they were wrong
without understanding
nothing to hold onto
but
holding tight
for a start
not now
then when

# Witness

caught up
in the inferno
only released
as a witness
innocent
and in fear
go slow
be careful
when
the time arrives
relief turns
to pride
or perhaps
not

# Anyone Can

loosing touch
calling out names
reaching for aide
who
be to the rescue
not a leader
not a follower
but a person
an average person
willing to try